Little Egg enjoys quiet strolls in the park.

Little Egg feels

CALM.

Little Egg likes to help others.

Little Egg feels **PROUD**.

Sometimes
Little Egg feels

ANGRY.

Other times
Little Egg feels

AFRAID.

All these emotions make Little Egg feel **confused**...

HAPPY CALM AFRAID
PROUD ANGRY
HAPPY CALM AFRAID
PROUD ANGRY

...and also a little bit

SAD.

But it's OK. All these feelings are normal.

Knowing this makes Little Egg feel

CONFIDENT...

...and

HAPPY.

Now it's your turn!